Popular Piano Solos
For All Piano Methods

LEVEL THREE 3

Table of Contents

Popular Piano Solos Level 3 is designed for use with the third book of any piano method.

Concepts in *Popular Piano Solos Level 3*:

Range

Symbols

pp, p, mp, mf, f, ff, ♯, ♭, ♮, ritard, a tempo

8va, ⌢, ℅, D.S. al Fine, ◁ ◁ ▷

simple pedaling

Rhythm

4/4 time signature

3/4 time signature

swing eighths

Intervals

2nd, 3rd, 4th, 5th, 6th melodic and harmonic

Three-note Chords

blocked and broken

ISBN 0-7935-7725-X

HAL•LEONARD® CORPORATION

7777 W. BLUEMOUND RD. P.O. BOX 13819 MILWAUKEE, WI 53213

Visit Hal Leonard Online at
www.halleonard.com

The Munster's Theme
from the Television Series

By Jack Marshall
Arranged by Bill Boyd

Spooky, medium fast

Accompaniment (Student plays one octave higher than written.)

Spooky, medium fast

Chim Chim Cher-ee
from Walt Disney's MARY POPPINS

Words and Music by Richard M. Sherman
and Robert B. Sherman
Arranged by Bill Boyd

Chim chim-in-ey chim chim-in-ey chim chim cher-ee! A sweep is as luck-y as luck-y can be.

Accompaniment (Student plays one octave higher than written.)

At The Hop

Words and Music by Arthur Singer,
John Madara and David White
Arranged by Mona Rejino

Accompaniment (Student plays one octave higher than written.)

Baby Elephant Walk

from the Paramount Picture HATARI!

By Henry Mancini
Arranged by Mona Rejino

Moderately, with a steady beat

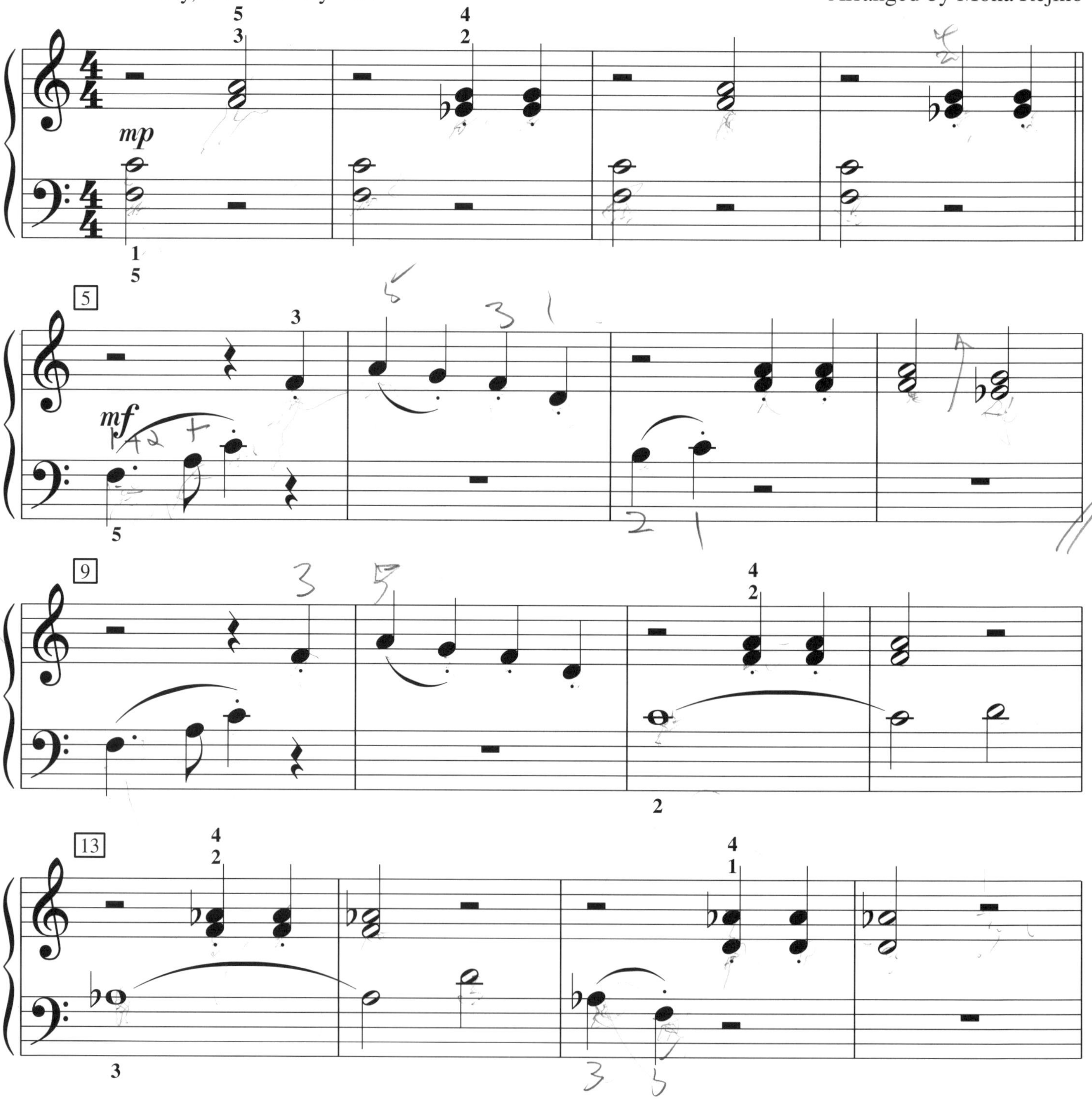

Accompaniment (Student plays one octave higher than written.) 7/8 4

Moderately, with a steady beat

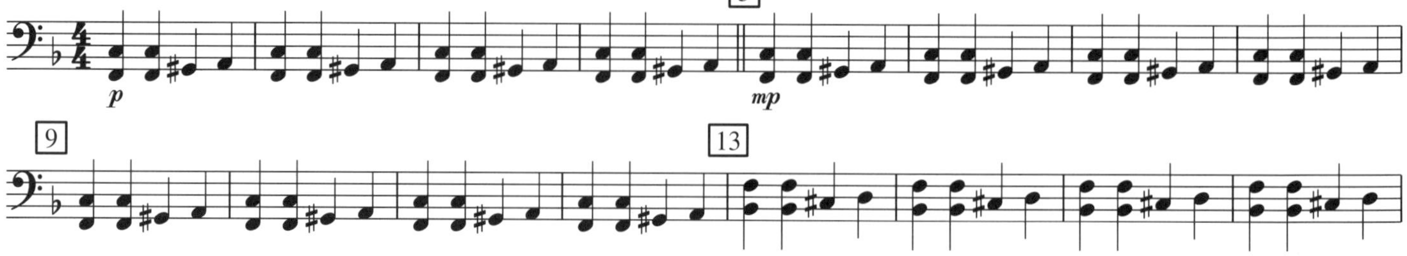

The Glory Of Love

Words and Music by
Billy Hill
Arranged by Bill Boyd

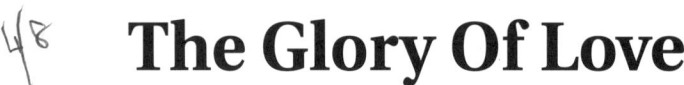

Easy going (Swing eighths)

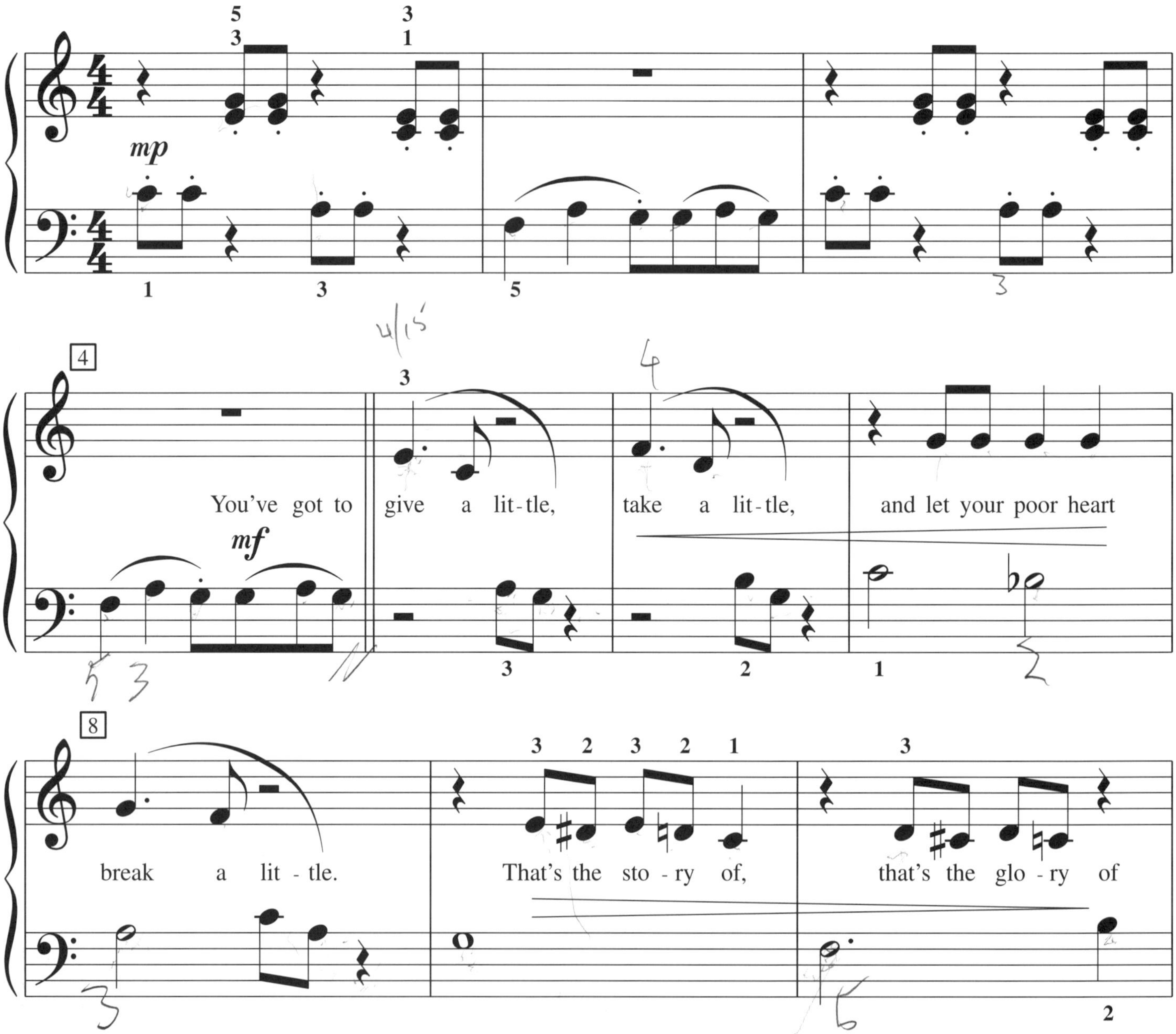
mp
You've got to give a lit-tle, take a lit-tle, and let your poor heart
mf
break a lit-tle. That's the sto-ry of, that's the glo-ry of

Accompaniment (Student plays one octave higher than written.) 9/10 5

Easy going

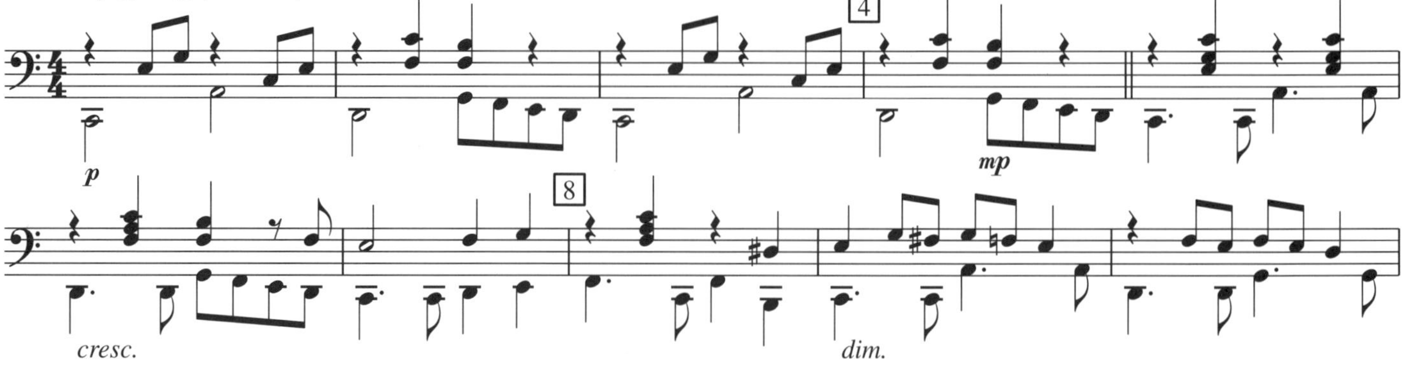
p
mp
cresc.
dim.

Yellow Submarine
from YELLOW SUBMARINE

Words and Music by John Lennon
and Paul McCartney
Arranged by Phillip Keveren

Bouncy March (Swing eighths)

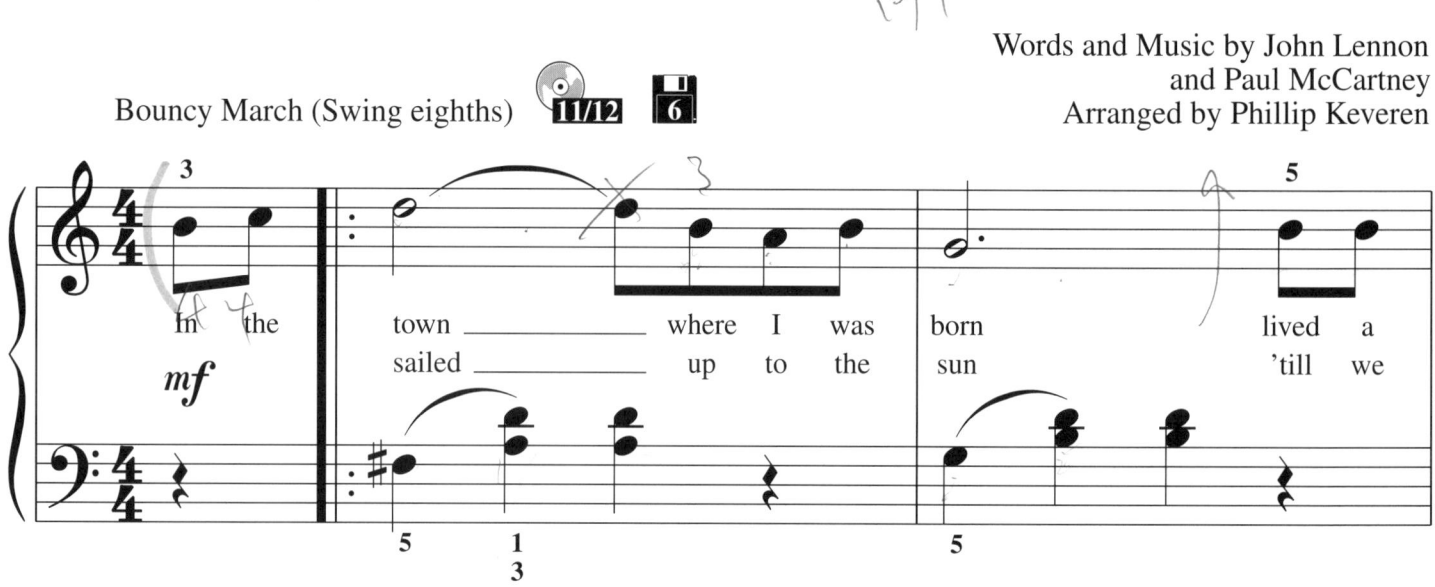

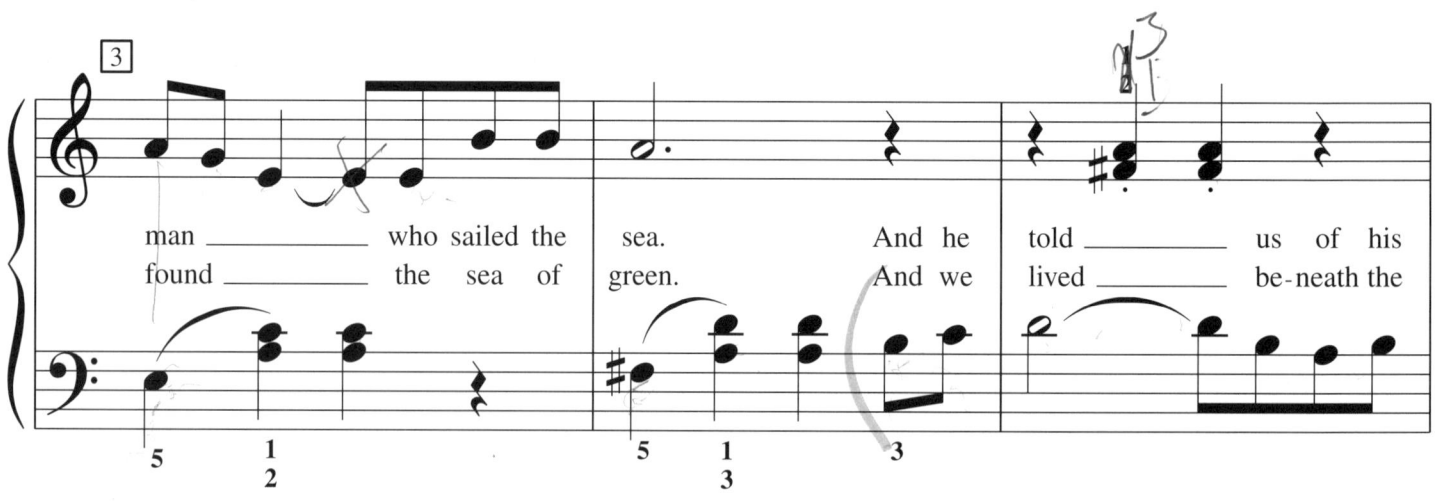

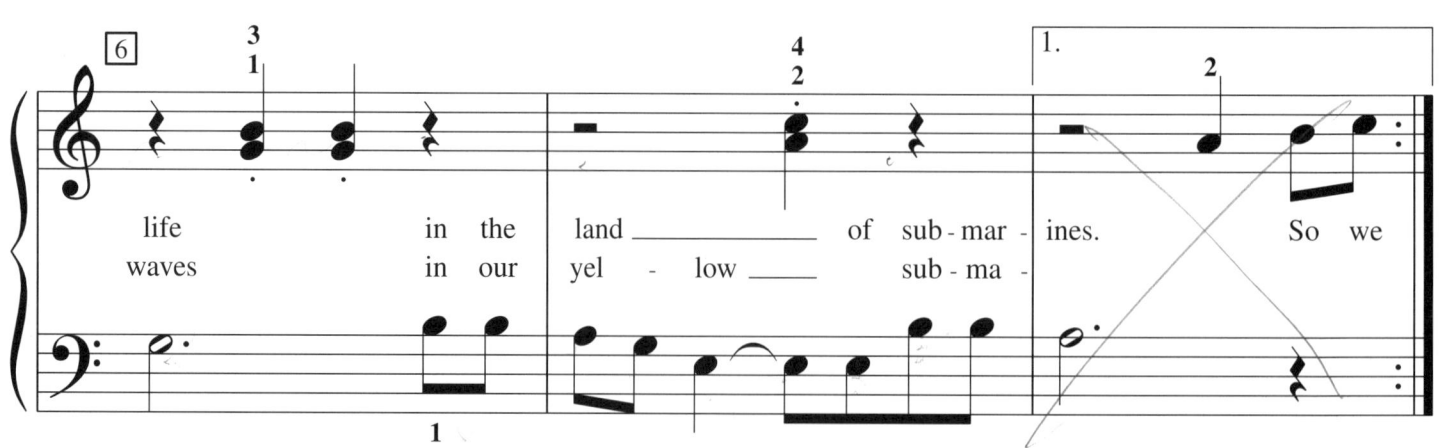

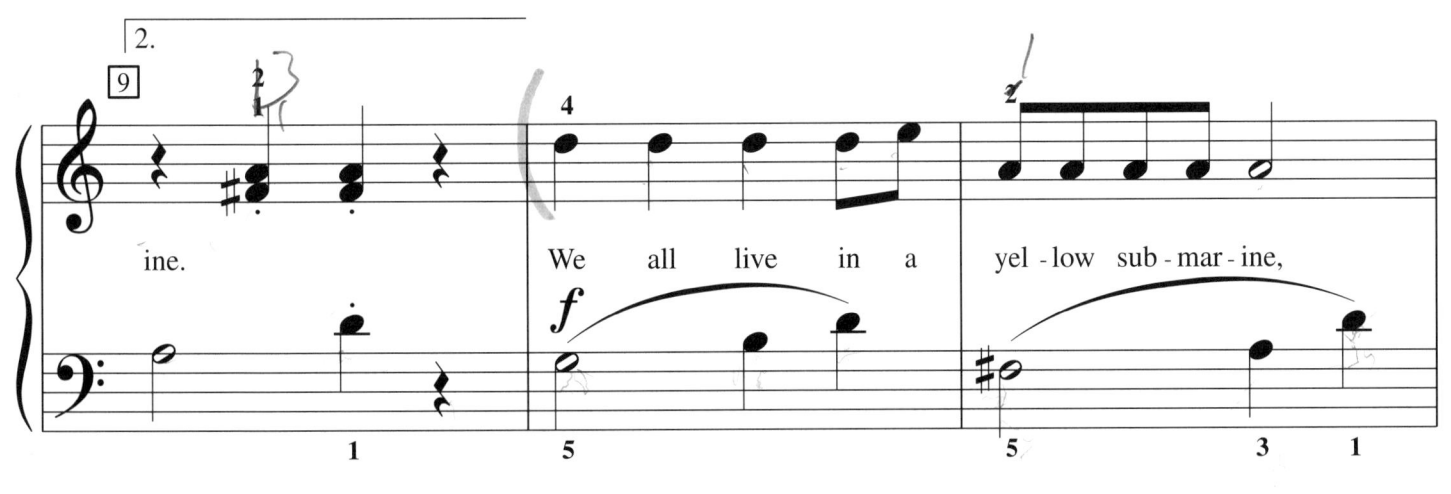

ine. We all live in a yel-low sub-mar-ine,

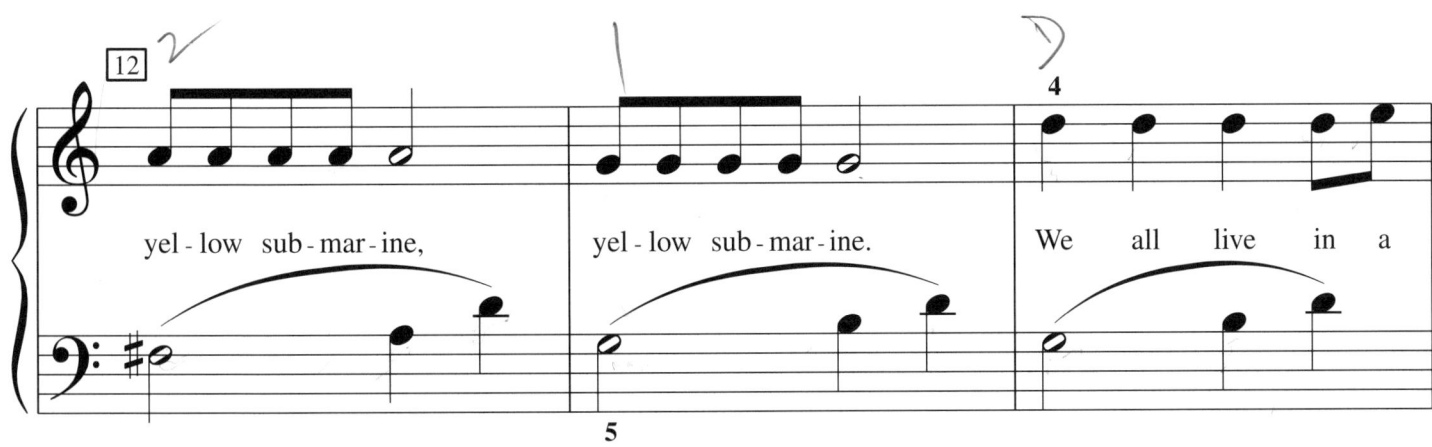

yel-low sub-mar-ine, yel-low sub-mar-ine. We all live in a

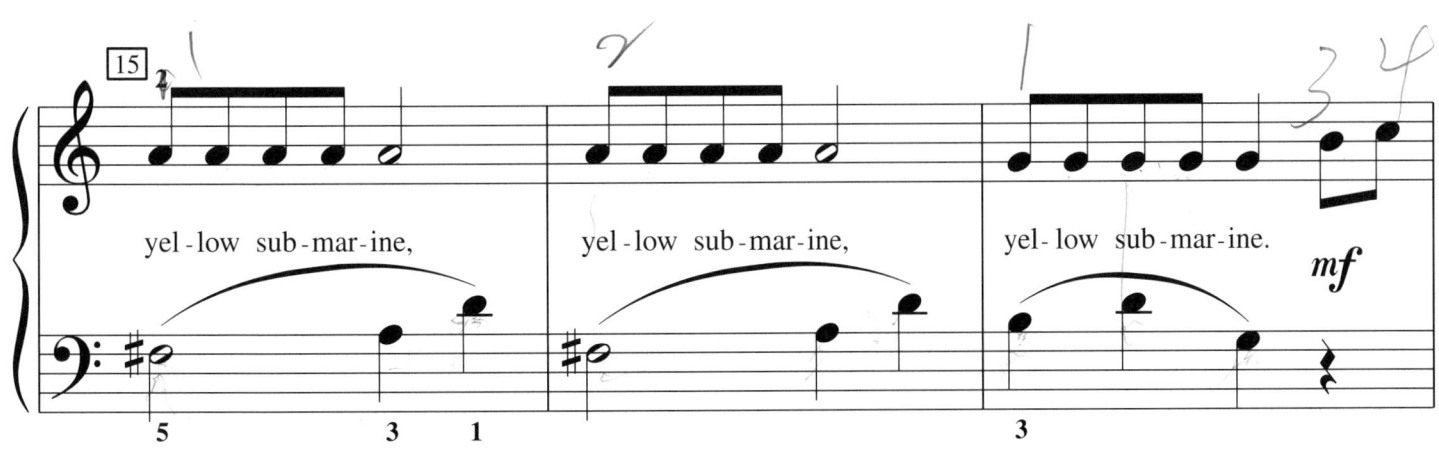

yel-low sub-mar-ine, yel-low sub-mar-ine, yel-low sub-mar-ine.

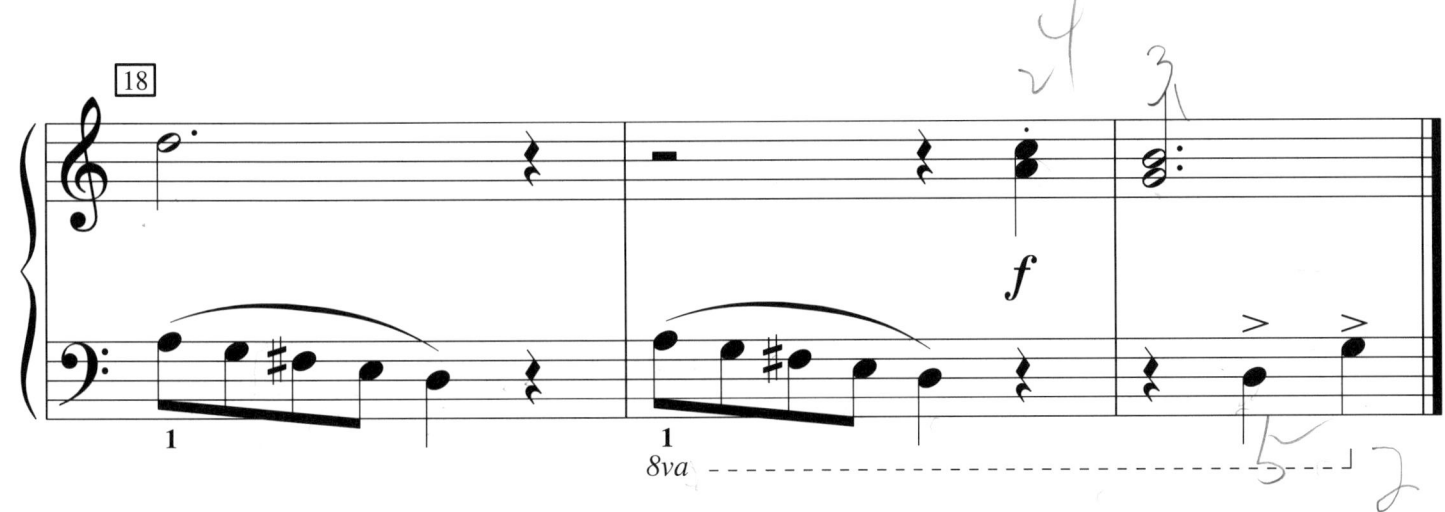

Raider's March
from the Paramount Motion Picture
RAIDERS OF THE LOST ARK

Majestic March

Music by John Williams
Arranged by Phillip Keveren

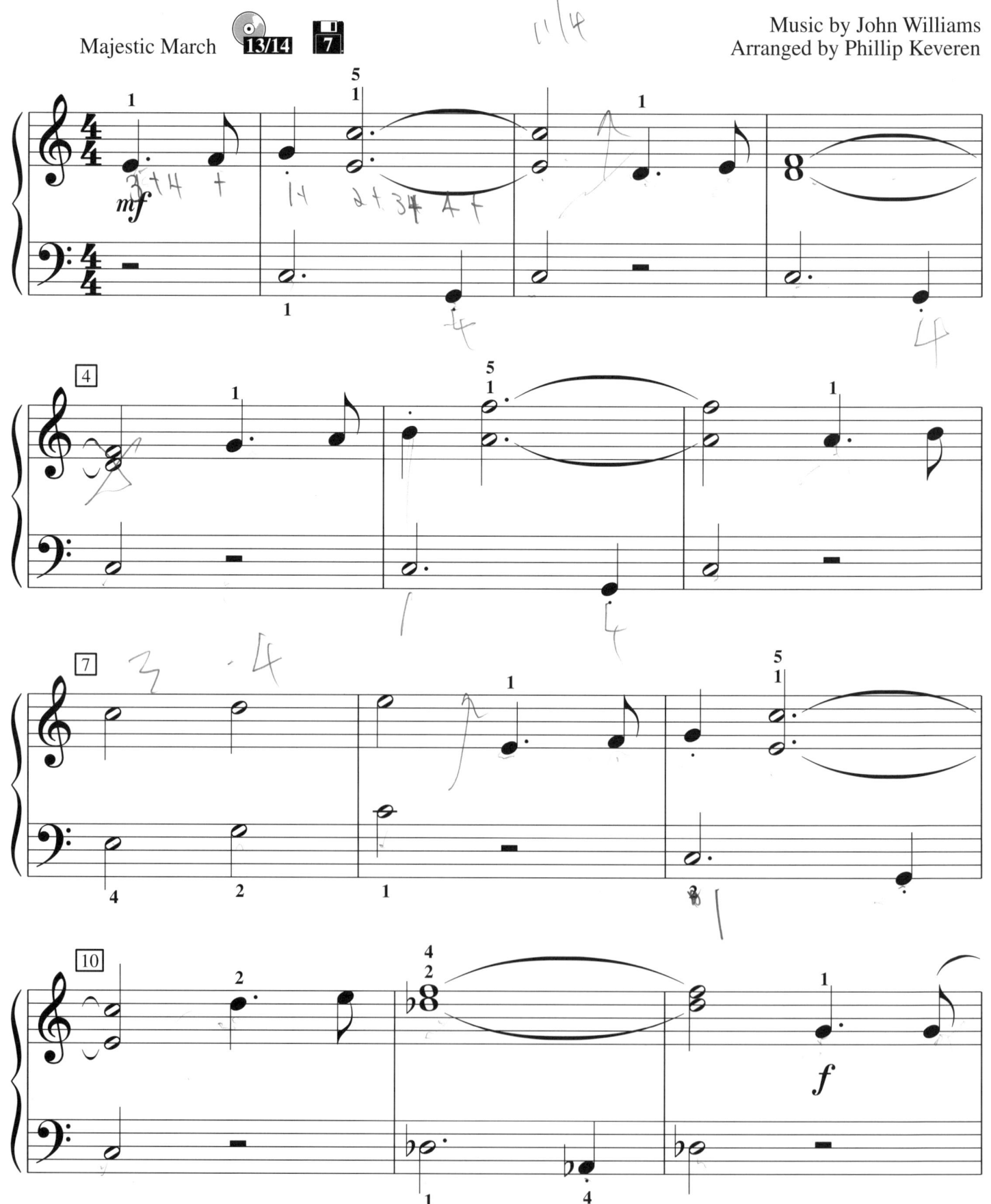

In The Mood

By Joe Garland
Arranged by Mona Rejino

Accompaniment (Student plays one octave higher than written.)

Beauty And The Beast
from Walt Disney's BEAUTY AND THE BEAST

Lyrics by Howard Ashman
Music by Alan Menken
Arranged by Robert Vandall

Lyrically

friends, then some-bod - y bends un - ex - pect - ed - ly.

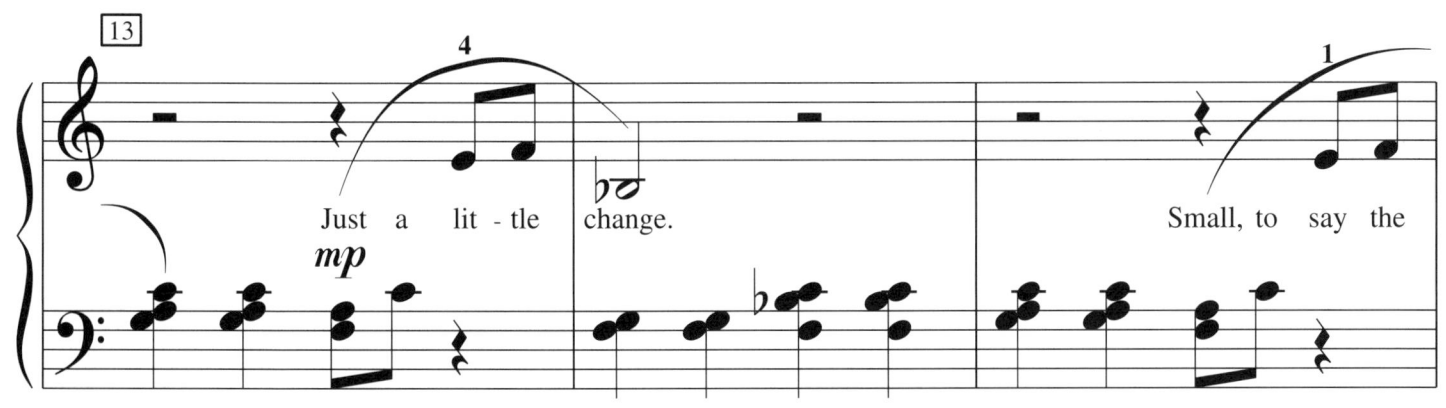

Just a lit - tle change. Small, to say the

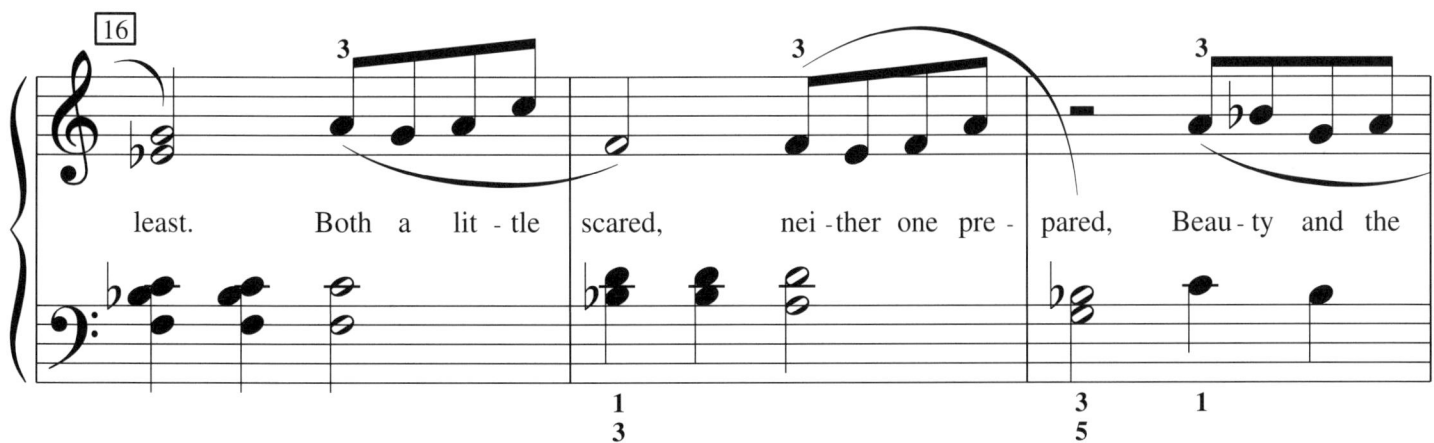

least. Both a lit - tle scared, nei - ther one pre - pared, Beau - ty and the

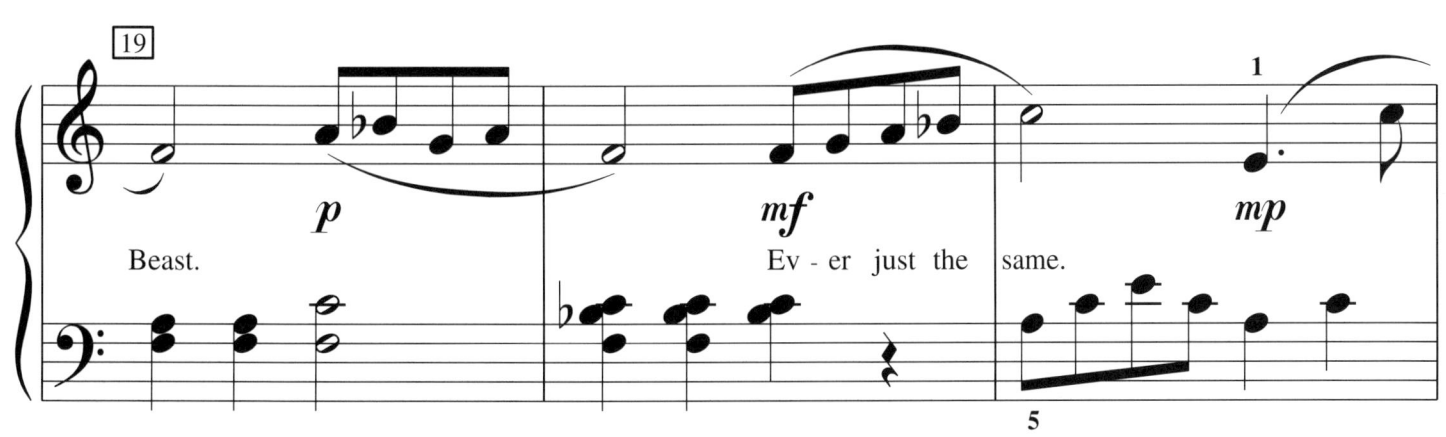

Beast. Ev - er just the same.

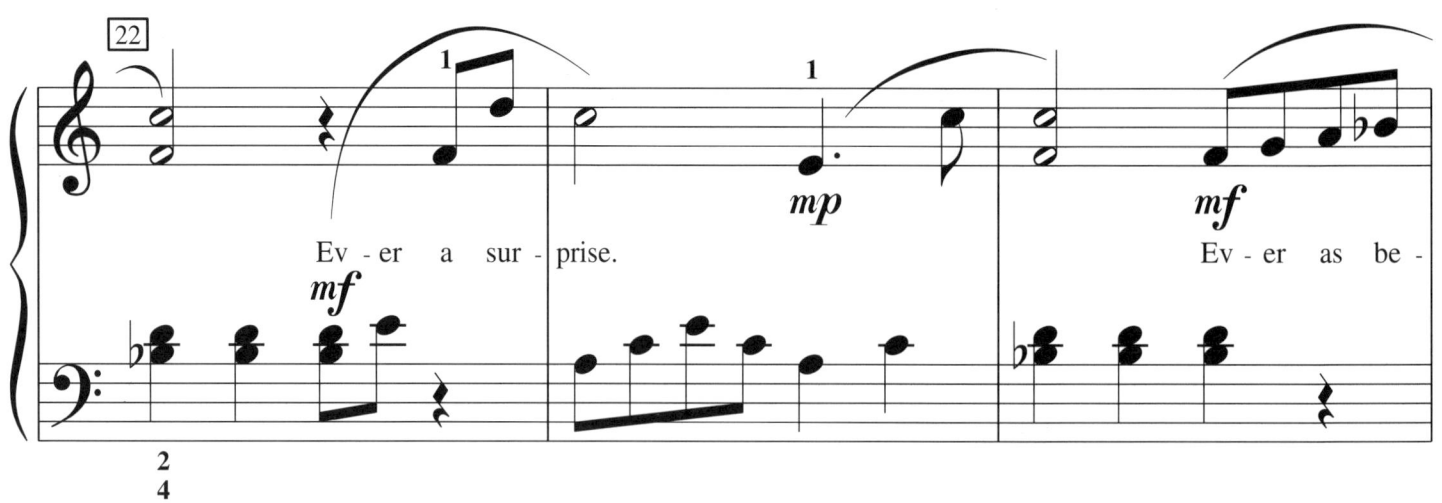

Ev - er a sur - prise. Ev - er as be -

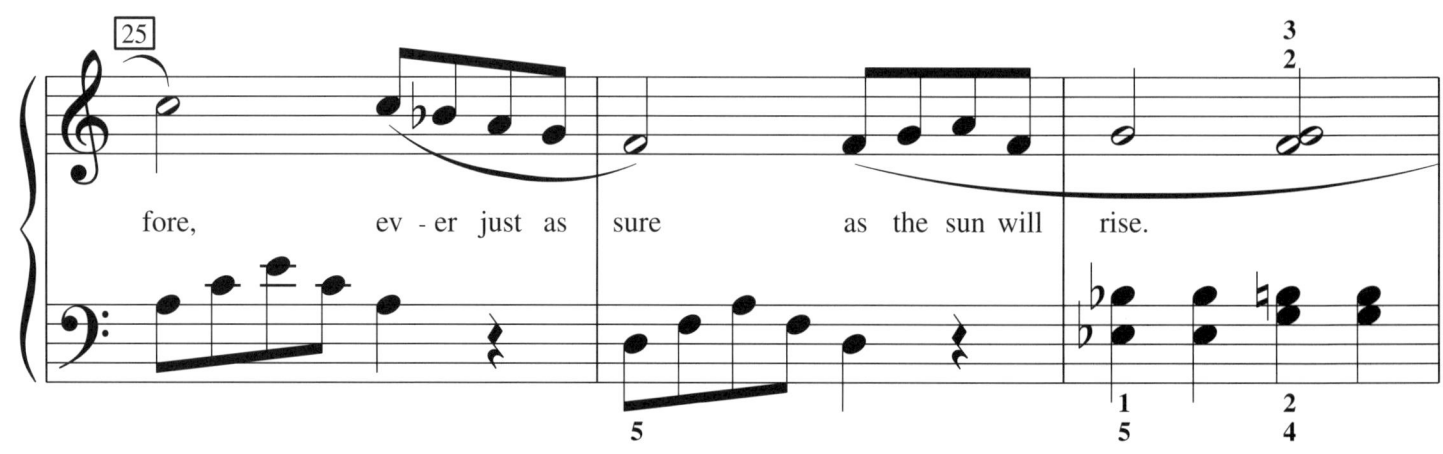

fore, ev - er just as sure as the sun will rise.

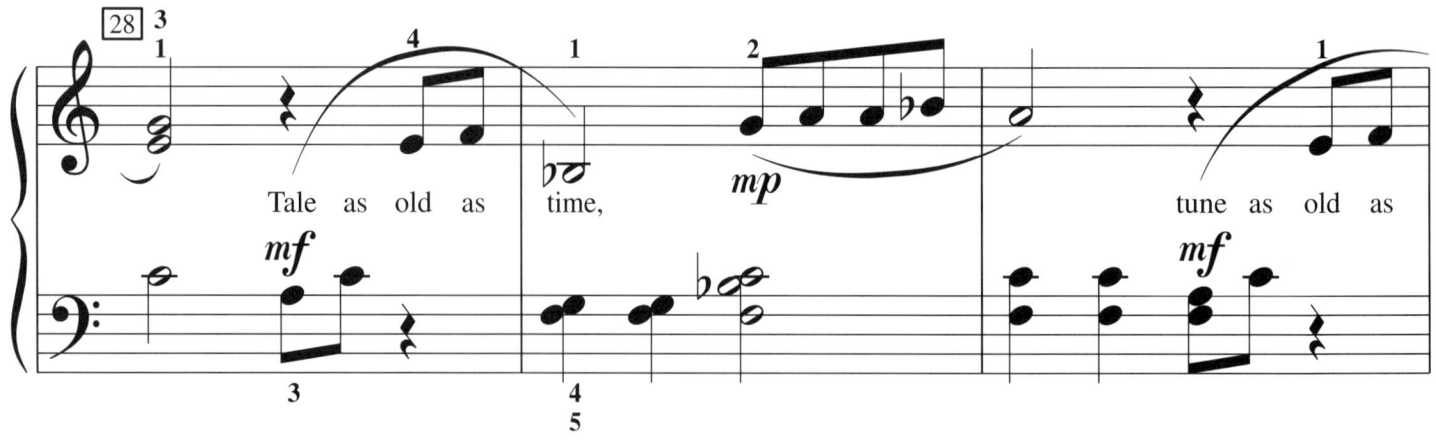

Tale as old as time, tune as old as

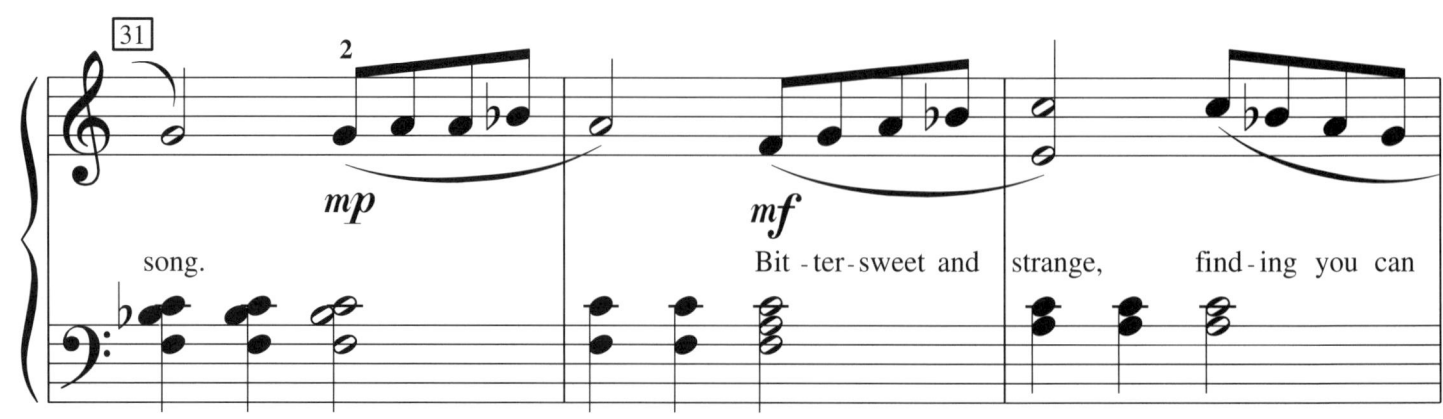

song. Bit - ter - sweet and strange, find - ing you can

Hal Leonard Student Piano Library

A piano method with music to please students, teachers and parents! The **Hal Leonard Student Piano Library** is clear, concise and carefully graded. Perfect for private and group instruction.

Piano Lessons 1-5
Appealing music introduces new concepts

Piano Lessons Instrumental Accompaniments 1-5
Correlated audio CD or General MIDI disk for lessons and games books

Piano Practice Games 1-4
Listening, reading, and improvisation activities correlated with lessons book

Notespeller for Piano 1-2
Note recognition activities

Piano Theory Workbook 1-5
Written theory activities correlated with lessons book

Piano Technique Book 1-5
Etudes to develop physical mastery of the keyboard (Instrumental Accompaniments optional)

Piano Solos 1-5
Additional correlated repertoire (Instrumental Accompaniments optional)

FOR MORE INFORMATION, SEE YOUR LOCAL MUSIC DEALER, OR WRITE TO:

HAL•LEONARD® CORPORATION

7777 W. BLUEMOUND RD. P.O. BOX 13819 MILWAUKEE, WI 53213